ISRAEL
IN PROPHECY

ISRAEL
IN PROPHECY

by WILLIAM HENDRIKSEN

BAKER BOOK HOUSE
Grand Rapids, Michigan

PHOTOLITHOPRINTED BY CUSHING - MALLOY, INC.
ANN ARBOR, MICHIGAN, UNITED STATES OF AMERICA
1974

CONTENTS

CHAPTER I

WHO KILLED JESUS?

When this question is asked many will immediately answer, "The Jews did." Today, however, a concerted effort is being made to absolve the Jews from any major responsibility for this act. It is readily understood, of course, that this effort is in line with the spirit of the ecumenical movement. The latter strives to make the church as all-inclusive as possible. In order to attain this end whatever might by some be interpreted as an unfriendly expression regarding any religious group must be carefully avoided. With respect to the Jews this means that the burden of blame for the death of Jesus must be lifted from their shoulders; if not entirely, at least as far as possible.

To a certain extent, the motive back of this effort merits approval. Throughout the centuries the proposition, "The Jews killed Jesus," has led to hatred of the Jews, anti-Semitism. Such an attitude is, of course, thoroughly un-Christian (see Matt. 5:7, 43-48; 6:14; 7:12; Luke 6:31-36; 23:34; Acts 7:60; Rom. 12:20; I Peter 2:23). Not only should it be avoided but it should be replaced by its very opposite.

This having been admitted, it must now be stated that in the process of showing kindness to the Jews we have no right to fly in the face of historical facts. What has happened cannot be changed. Justice demands that blame be fixed where Scripture places it. In the end this will prove to be an act not only of fairness but even of kindness, and this even toward the Jews.

During the past two decades the business of blunting the sharp edge of accusations against the Jews has made important progress. As to the result? Some of it is undoubtedly good; some questionable. Here are some excerpts from public declarations regarding this matter:

The First Assembly of the Protestant World Council of Churches, Amsterdam, 1948, declared: "Before our churches can hope to fulfil the commission laid upon us by our Lord there are high barriers to be overcome. . . . We call upon all the churches we represent to denounce anti-Semitism, no matter what its origin, as absolutely irreconcilable with the profession and practice of the Christian faith. Anti-Semitism is sin against God and man." To this we can only say, "Amen!"

The Third Assembly, New Delhi, 1961, issued the following statement: "In Christian teaching the historic events which led to the Crucifixion should not be so presented as to fasten upon the Jewish people today the responsibilities which belong to our corporate humanity and not to one race or community. Jews were the first to accept Jesus and Jews are not the only ones who do not recognize him." That this is a biased statement is clear on the very surface.

The New Delhi declaration is deficient at least in the following respects: (a) In fixing blame or absolving from blame it fails to base its declaration on any reliable source. There is, for example, no appeal to Scripture. (b) Granted that in connection with Christ's death there are, indeed, "responsibilities which belong to our corporate humanity" (Rom. 5: 12-19), *that* is not the whole of the story. As will be pointed out later, there is also concrete, historical blame, which Scripture places squarely upon the Jews who crucified the Lord. (c) As will be pointed out, even "the Jewish people *today,*" if they approve of, acquiesce in, and/or continue in the sins of their ancestors, must share the blame. (d) The statement that "Jews were the first to accept Jesus" is onesided, for it remains true that by and large they were also the very ones who in large numbers *rejected* him (Matt. 27:25; John 1:11; 6:66).

Passing over additional resolutions (all of them in the year 1964) by the National Council of Churches of Christ ("We have even used the events of the Crucifixion to condemn the Jewish people . . .”), by the Lutheran World Federation, and by the House of Bishops of the Protestant Episcopal Church, we shall now quote an excerpt from *The Declaration on the Jews by the Second Vatican Council, 1965.*

Before doing so, however, it is necessary to say something with respect to the origin of this Vatican decree. It arose out of an earlier "schema," which aroused considerable opposition. As interpreted by many, this schema went too far in the direction of exonerating the Jews from all responsibility for the death of Christ. At any rate this *proposal* presented by a *committee* is not the same as an official *decision* by *the council.* It is said that Pope Paul VI himself exerted considerable influence in bringing about what many regard as a more biblical reformulation. Insofar as this reworded declaration states that the Jewish authorities and those who followed their lead pressed for the death of Jesus, but that the Jews should not be persecuted, it is hard to see how anyone can disagree with it. However, when it states that Christ's crucifixion cannot be charged against the Jews of today, the answer is that although today's Jews cannot be charged with *direct, historical* responsibility for the plot to crucify the Lord, for they were not even present at that time, yet by means of their unconcern about this death and their continued rejection of the Christ, they have arrayed themselves on the side of those who perpetrated this crime! And in that sense it is entirely scriptural to speak of (a) the Jews who bitterly opposed the Lord and (b) those who now oppose his followers, as being, indeed, *one* people, on whom, as long as they continue in this obstinate refusal to acknowledge and forsake their sins and to accept Christ as their Savior, God's marked disapproval rests (I Thess. 2:14, 15; cf. Rom. 11:7-10, 25). It is for this reason that the sentiment expressed in the following excerpt from the official Roman Catholic declaration must be regarded as being too weak; hence, as being not entirely in harmony with Scripture:

"True, the Jewish authorities and those who followed their lead pressed for the death of Christ (cf. John 19:6); still, what happened in his passion cannot be charged against all the Jews, without distinction, then alive, nor against the Jews of today. Although the Church is the new People of God, the Jews should not be represented as rejected by God or accursed, as if this followed from the holy Scriptures."

Immediately after the publication of this historic declaration the following streamer-headline appeared in various newspapers:

VATICAN ABSOLVES JEWS OF CRUCIFIXION BLAME

Though this version was hardly true to fact, it is easy to understand how it arose. The sharp edge of Scripture's language had again been blunted sufficiently to account for this misinterpretation.

Moreover, the Jews themselves, as could be expected, have gone even farther in absolving themselves from blame. In a recent issue of *Israel Law Review* the Israel Supreme Court Justice Haim Cohn, an internationally famous specialist in Jewish legal tradition, argues that not only did the Jews take no part in the trial of Jesus, but also that the Sanhedrin, Judaism's high court, actually did its level best to save Jesus from death! As Cohn sees it, the men of this court tried to persuade Jesus to plead *not guilty* before the Romans. Jesus refused, however. It was accordingly his own fault that he was subsequently sentenced by Pilate. When Pilate asked him "Are *you* the king of the Jews?" he answered, "You said so," which in effect was a *nolo contendere* (I do not wish to contest it) admission of guilt. Therefore he was crucified for the self-confessed crime of sedition.

Now this notion, that the Sanhedrin actually tried to save Jesus, collides with everything the Bible tells us about the attitude which this supreme council took toward Jesus (Matt.

26:59; 27:18; Mark 14:55; 15:1, 10; Luke 22:66; John 9:22, 23; 11:46-50; 12:42). Completely contrary to Scripture is also the opinion that Jesus ever admitted guilt in connection with the charge of inciting rebellion against the Roman government. Even a *nolo contendere, if* this were a legitimate interpretation of Matt. 27:11 or of John 18:37, would not necessarily imply confession of guilt. But any intelligent reader can see that, in admitting that he is a king, Jesus is speaking about his *spiritual* kingship, his royal rule in the hearts of all those who love and obey the truth. Even Pilate sensed this, and therefore was not at all convinced that Christ's claim to kingship was fraught with danger to the Roman government. Accordingly, the governor declared, "No crime whatever do I find in him" (John 18:38; cf. Matt. 27:23; Mark 15:14; Luke 23:4).

Hence, the only way in which the Jews are able to invest the deed of their ancestors with even a semblance of fairness is by denying the trustworthiness of the New Testament records. These records do, indeed, charge the Jews with responsibility for the death of Jesus. To the credit of some of the leading Jews of the present generation it must be said that they admit this. Haim Cohn, for one, rejects much of what the Gospels tell us about the trial of Jesus. He knows that he *must* do so in order to pronounce the Jews free from guilt. And another Jew, Hugh J. Schonfield, though differing with Cohn on some points, agrees with him in rejecting the veracity of the narrative set forth by the evangelists. He calls the charge that the Jewish people were responsible for the death of Jesus "an antisemitic fraud," and then immediately states that the only way for the church once and for all to remove the stigma from the Jews is to renounce the absolute reliability of its sacred documents (*The Passover Plot,* p. 142; cf. p. 140).

The only sources that can be depended upon in our search for an answer to the question whether or not the Jews killed Jesus are those found in Scripture. Now when the veracity of these documents — Matthew, Mark, Luke, John, Acts, etc. — is admitted, the following points become clear:

1. *Gravest responsibility for the death of Jesus rests, indeed, on the Jewish leaders. Their guilt was greater than that of the Gentile Pilate.*

There are those today who teach the very opposite. They hold that not the Jews but the Gentiles were, or were *chiefly,* responsible for this death. But it was Jesus himself who said to Pilate, "The one who delivered me to you has greater sin" (John 19:11). There are gradations in sin (Luke 12:47, 58). To whom much is given, from him much will be required. Pilate, the Gentile, was certainly guilty. He was proud (John 19:10), cruel (Luke 13:1), and superstitious (John 19:8; cf. Matt. 27:19). Above all, he was unscrupulous, *a self-seeker.* But not being a Jew, he had not been instructed in the oracles of the one true God, nor had he shared with the Jews the opportunity, day by day, week after week, to watch the deeds and to hear the words of Jesus. But the case of the Jewish leaders was entirely different. To them much had been given. Take, for example, Annas and his son-in-law Caiaphas. Not only had they been instructed in the Old Testament but they had also had abundant opportunity to reflect on the claims of Jesus in the light of his mighty and merciful deeds and of Old Testament prophecy. Yet they hardened their hearts in the face of all this evidence. Annas (or Ananus, as Josephus calls him) had been appointed high priest by Quirinius in the year A.D. 6. He was deposed by Valerius Gratus about A.D. 15. But though deposed, and accordingly no longer legally the high priest and president of the Sanhedrin at the time of Jesus' trial and death, he remained the dominant member of the Jewish hierarchical machine. He was the power behind the throne. Five sons and a grandson succeeded him in the high priesthood; also, as stated above, a son-in-law, Caiaphas. The latter occupied the high-priestly office during the days of Christ's passion. But whoever might be the presiding officer of the Sanhedrin, Annas was still the man to consult. One can imagine how, whenever a priest would come up with a plan or idea, and would broach it, another would immediately reply, "Have you cleared this with Annas?" He was proud, ambitious, and wealthy. His family was notorious for its greed. His wealth was derived, in part, from the exorbitant profits realized from the sale of sacrificial animals which could be purchased by the worshippers in the temple, that is, in its Court of the Gentiles. By him and his relatives the house of prayer had been turned into "a den of robbers." Upon greedy, serpent-like, vindictive Annas, upon rude, sly, hypocritical Caiaphas (cf. John 11:49, 50), and upon others of their kind, men filled with envy (Matt. 27:18) because of Christ's mighty deeds and the people's resulting applause (John 11:47, 48), the responsibility for the plot to kill Jesus *mainly* rests. It was they whose greed had been exposed by means of Christ's temple-cleansing(s). The *leaders* — chief priests and elders — *"persuaded* the multitudes that they should ask for [the release of] Barabbas, and *destroy Jesus"* (Matt. 27:20).

2. *Accordingly, the guilt of the leaders was also greater than that of the Jewish people as a whole.* The multitudes, to be sure, permitted themselves to be persuaded, but the leaders did the persuading.

Not the masses but the leaders — chief priests, Pharisees, Caiaphas — are mentioned in John 11:53 as the ones who plotted Christ's death. Jesus uttered his *Seven Woes* (Matt. 23) not against the mob but against "scribes and Pharisees, hypocrites." When Pilate at Jesus' trial said to the multitude, "I am bringing him out to you in order that you may know that I find no crime in him," it was the chief priests and their officers who shouted "Crucify (him), crucify (him)" (John 19:6; cf. verses 15, 16). Here, too, the priest-ridden mob *follows the example* of its leaders, as Matt. 27:20-23 makes very clear.

3. *Nevertheless, by no means is it possible, on scriptural grounds, entirely to excuse the Jewish people as a whole, as if only their leaders were guilty. All those who took part in the crime or were in agreement with it must share the blame.*

The following passages make this point abundantly clear:

"And all the people answered and said, His blood be on us and on our children" (Matt. 27:25).

"Truly in this city there were gathered together against thy holy servant Jesus, whom thou didst anoint, both Herod and Pontius Pilate, with the Gentiles and the peoples of Israel" (Acts 4:27; cf. 3:13-15).

"The Jews . . . killed the Lord Jesus" (I Thess. 2:14, 15).

Accordingly, on the basis of Holy Writ one is fully justified in declaring that it actually was the Jews who killed Jesus. This firm belief, moreover, is not a manifestation of hostility toward Jews (anti-Semitism). The very opposite is the truth. It is because we love the Jews that we desire to become the means in God's hand to bring them to Christ, *and thus also into the fellowship of the church!* We *feel* for these people. In fact *in a sense,* we stand where they stand, for we made common cause with them against Jesus. Not that we plotted his death, as did *their* ancestors. Yet it remains true that we, yes even we ourselves, killed Jesus, for our sins nailed him to the cross. But by that very crucified and risen Christ we were saved.

Moreover, because we love the Jews, may God Almighty prevent us from harming them! We would be cruel to them were we to tell them that their ancestors did not kill Jesus and/or that they themselves can afford to be cold or indifferent with respect to Christ's death. We shall not do this. On the contrary, with the apostle Peter we say to the Jews, "Let all the house of Israel therefore know beyond the shadow of a doubt that God has made him both Lord and Christ, namely, this very Jesus whom you crucified" (Acts 2:36). And we shall strive, by the grace and power of the Lord, to impress upon them that for them as well as for ourselves and for every truly penitent sinner there is power in the blood of the Lamb. God grant that genuine sorrow may pierce also *their* hearts, so that they, too, may seek and find him who will *abundantly* pardon.

"Who was the guilty? Who brought this upon thee?
Alas, *my* treason, Jesus, hath undone thee!
'Twas I, Lord Jesus, I it was denied thee;
I crucified thee.

"Therefore, dear Jesus, since I cannot pay thee,
I do adore thee, and will ever pray thee,
Think on *thy* pity and *thy* love unswerving,
Not *my* deserving."

> Stanzas from "Ah, Dearest Jesus,"
> by Johann Heermann,
> tr. by Robert Bridges

CHAPTER II

ARE "THE RESTORATION OF THE JEWS" PROPHECIES BEING FULFILLED TODAY?

It is a rather common belief among Christians of various faiths that the recent return of many Jews to Palestine and their establishment as an independent state May 14, 1948, is a fulfilment of prophecy.[1] This opinion, *with many variations as to details,* is set forth in the following brief twelve-point summary. *Let it be stated at the outset that this summary does not represent the conviction of the author of this treatise, and, having been given, will be refuted point by point.*

A. Summary

1. The return itself is even now a partial reality. It will be completed in the not too distant future. Proof: "And I will bring back your captivity [or: will restore your fortune], and I will gather you from all the nations, and from all the places whither I have driven you, says Jehovah; and I will bring you again to the place whence I have banished you" (Jer. 29:14).

2. Since this return is described as a going back *not only from Shinar or Babylon* but "from all the nations and from all the places" of the dispersion (Jer. 29:14), "from Assyria and from Egypt and from . . . Shinar . . . and from the four corners of the earth" (Isa. 11:11, 12), it must refer to what is happening today and is still to take place in the future.

3. This is not the first return but the second one (Isa. 11: 11).

4. Since these return prophecies are at times addressed to

---

[1]See, for example, G. T. B. Davis, "Regathering Israel — A Modern Miracle," *The Sunday School Times* (March 19, 1949); R. Wolff, *Israel Act III,* 1967, pp. 43-49. Also see footnote 3.

people who had already come back from the Babylonian captivity (Zech. 8:1-8), they must refer to later happenings, that is, to twentieth century events and others.

5. The expression "in the latter days" (Jer. 30:24) confirms this.

6. The predicted return is "in unbelief" (Ezek. 36:24-26), which agrees with what is happening today.[2]

7. The establishment of the state of Israel on May 14, 1948, is proof of the fact that these ancient prophecies are being fulfilled.[3]

8. Hand in hand with political re-establishment goes physical and economic restoration. Did not Isaiah predict that one day the desert would rejoice and blossom as the rose [or crocus] and that the ancient ruins would be rebuilt (Isa. 35:1; 61:4)? Accordingly, prophecy is being fulfilled today in the reclamation of the soil after centuries of neglect, in the diversion of water from the Jordan to irrigate the Negev desert, in the building of numerous new cities and villages, in the re-utilization of long-forgotten physical resources, and so on. Travel advertising is therefore justified in taking advantage of this situation. See, for example, the ad in *Christianity Today*, October 27, 1967: "Is Prophecy Being Fulfilled In The Bible Lands Today? Come and See."

9. In fulfilment of Amos 9:14, 15,[4] the swift victories of the Jews over their enemies — May, 1948, October, 1956, and especially June, 1967[5] — prove that God's promises to Israel are being — and will be — fulfilled, and that it will be impossible to eradicate the state of Israel.

---

[2]See H. Bultema, *Maranatha*, p. 83; J. M. Grey, *Prophecy and the Lord's Return*, p. 23; R. Wolff, *op. cit.*, pp. 44, 45.

[3]"The re-establishment of that nation in its own land, even in unbelief, is significant indeed," *Voice of the Independent Fundamental Churches of America*, August, 1949.

[4]R. Wolff, *op. cit.*, pp. 3, 13, 44, 62.

[5]See the magazine *Newsweek* (June 5, 1967, p. 43; June 19, 1967, pp. 24-30).

10. The return of the ancient city of Jerusalem to the custody of the Jews proves that the prophecy of Luke 21:24, namely, "Jerusalem will be trodden down by the Gentiles until the times of the Gentiles are fulfilled," has now gone into fulfilment, for Jerusalem is no longer being trodden down by them.[6]

Probably implied in Paul's teaching is the prediction that the Jews, having returned, will rebuild the temple. Antichrist will take his seat in this literally rebuilt temple (II Thess. 2:4).[7] This prediction, too, may be in the process of being fulfilled. In fact, if reports are reliable, loads of stone, precut to exact specifications for this rebuilding, are already being sent to Israel.[8]

11. Among other New Testament passages that point in the direction of the end-of-the-age restoration of the Jews (national return in unbelief followed by national conversion) is especially Matt. 19:28, which clearly teaches the regathering of the twelve tribes.

12. Finally, there is also I Cor. 10:32 which, in making mention of the Jews and the church as the two groups on which God bestows his special favor, as contrasted with the third group, "the Gentiles" (Authorized Version), clearly indicates "that God still has a program for Israel."

Galatians 6:6 ("and upon the Israel of God") and Rom. 11:26 ("and so all Israel shall be saved") will be treated separately, in Chapter III.

B. *Refutation*

The author of the treatise which you are reading regards this entire presentation to be an error. As he sees it, these

---

[6]See the well-written and in many respects valuable insert by W. M. Smith, "The Second Advent of Christ," p. 19, included in the December 22, 1967 issue of *Christianity Today*.

[7]R. Wolff, *op. cit.,* pp. 13, 62-64.

[8]See "Israel: Things To Come," *Christianity Today* (December 22, 1967), p. 35.

ancient prophecies, whether Old or New Testament, do not refer to recent or coming events.

Taking up the above-mentioned points one by one, the answer is as follows:

Answer to 1. The context of the Jer. 29:14 passage speaks specifically of a return "after seventy years" (Jer. 29:10), correctly interpreted by Daniel (in his book, 9:2), as applying to the time in which he was living. It cannot be proved, therefore, that such a passage has anything to do with recent or still future migrations. The same holds, of course, for similar restoration passages, such as Deut. 30:1-10; I Kings 8:46-52; Ezek. 36:17-19, 26-28; Hos. 11:10, 11.

Answer to 2. The fact that, in addition to Shinar (Babylonia), several other countries and regions are also mentioned as places from which Jews were to return, presents no difficulty, if only it be remembered that it was customary in those days to sell some of the war-prisoners to nations round about, so that they were dispersed far and wide (Ezek. 27:13; Joel 3:7; Amos 1:6, 9; Rev. 18:13). In the step-by-step return from captivity — now some returning, later others, and afterward still others — it is natural that also some of these widely dispersed Jews went back to the Promised Land, the country from which they or their ancestors had come. It is well-known that the slave-trade was carried on especially by the Phoenicians whose mariners pushed boldly out to various parts of the then-known world, selling their "merchandise," which included slaves. Moreover, the fact that, here in Isa. 11:11, in the enumeration of the nations of the dispersion Assyria and Egypt are mentioned first is again very natural, for how often had not the prophets, especially Isaiah, warned the people to lean neither on Assyria nor on Egypt! And how often had not the people placed their trust *now* in Egypt, *then* in Assyria, constantly shifting their allegiance from the one to the other, instead of committing themselves, without any reservation, to the care of Jehovah! Not only here in Isa. 11:11 but

also elsewhere these two — Assyria and Egypt — are mentioned together (Isa. 7:18; 19:24, 25; 20:4; 27:13; Jer. 2:36,
37; Hos. 7:11; Zech. 10:10; etc.). From all these regions,
therefore, Jews, in greater or lesser numbers, were to return.
There is no reason whatever to doubt that this is also what
actually took place. Moreover, those who returned did not
belong exclusively to the tribe of Judah (or to Judah and
Benjamin) but also, to some extent, to the other ten tribes.
See I Chron. 9:33, 34; Ezra 2:59. When during the reign of
Darius the temple was rebuilt and dedicated, a sin-offering was
brought "*for all Israel,* twelve he-goats, according to the number of the tribes of Israel" (Ezra 6:17). This is also the New
Testament view. It looks upon Israel as a reunited people,
consisting of "twelve tribes," whether literally or symbolically
conceived (Matt. 19:28; Acts 26:7; James 1:1; Rev. 7:1-8;
21:12). In connection with the story of the birth of John the
Baptist and of Jesus we read not only about Joseph and Mary
of the tribe of Judah (II Sam. 7:12, 13; Matt. 1:20; Luke 1:27;
2:4, 5; Acts 2:30; Rom. 1:3; II Tim. 2:8; Rev. 5:5), but also
of Zechariah and Elizabeth of the tribe of Levi (Exod. 2:1;
4:14; I Chron. 24:1, 10; Luke 1:5), and of Anna, a prophetess,
of the tribe of Asher (Luke 2:36). Over all the tribes, now
viewed as *one* people, rules the *one* Shepherd, according to
prophecy (Ezek. 37:15-28). Says G. Ch. Aalders, "To be sure,
in the return from the Babylonian captivity the emphasis falls
on Judah, but by no means are the ten tribes excluded. They
probably took a more prominent part in this return than many
people think."[9]

It has become clear, therefore, that there is no reason whatever for interpreting Isa. 11:11, 12, *in its literal application,*
as referring to what is taking place in the twentieth century
A.D. On the contrary, that view is open to serious objection:
In the context we are told that those who have returned from
the captivity "will swoop down upon the shoulder of the
Philistines to the west, will together plunder the people of the

---

[9]*Het Herstel van Israel volgens het Oude Testament,* p. 44.

east, and will put forth their hand against Edom and Moab. The children of Ammon will obey them" (Isa. 11:14). That these predictions were fulfilled is clear from I Macc. 3:41; 5:1-8, 68; 10:83-89; 11:60, 61; etc. However, those who believe that *now*, in the twentieth century A.D., these Philistines, Edomites, Moabites, and Ammonites must still be destroyed or plundered or subjected will have a hard time even *finding* them!

Answer to 3. The fact that Isa. 11:11 refers to a *second* recovery has nothing whatever to do with recent events, for according to the context the *first* recovery or exodus was the one under Moses. It was the return from the house of bondage (Isa. 11:16). Hence, the second recovery was fulfilled when, in stages, the Jews returned from the Assyrian-Babylonian captivity, and were established in their own land. All this took place long, long ago. There is, accordingly, no justification for interpreting these prophecies as if they referred to events happening in the twentieth century A.D.

Answer to 4. The same thing holds with respect to predictions made to those who had already returned. Zechariah carried on his prophetic activity about the year 520 B.C. His divinely inspired prophecy of a still further return of exiles, and of a restoration of peaceful life in Jerusalem, old men and women dwelling in it, and boys and girls playing in its streets (Zech. 8:1-8), was fulfilled in the days of Ezra, Nehemiah, and afterward. See Ezra 7:1-10; Neh. 11:1, 2; I Macc. 14:8-12.

Answer to 5. The expression "the latter days" (Jer. 30:24) occurs also in the following passages: Gen. 49:1; Num. 24:14; Deut. 4:30; 31:29; Isa. 2:2; Jer. 23:20; 48:47; 49:39; Ezek. 38:16; Dan. 10:14; Hos. 3:5; Micah 4:1. In each instance its meaning must be interpreted in the light of the specific context. That this phrase does not necessarily have any reference to Christ's second coming or to the days immediately preceding that event is clear from its very first occurrence (Gen. 49:1). Jacob was not trying to tell his sons what would happen *to them* — note "what will befall *you*" — *in the twentieth century A.D.!* He predicted what would take place during the lifetime of his children and of their descendants in days to come. To be sure, even the *first* coming of Christ out of the tribe of Judah is included in these predictions (Gen. 49:10), but nothing whatever is mentioned here regarding the days of Christ's *second* coming. And as to the twelve tribes, in their separate existence, where are they today? Accordingly, the translation of Gen. 49:10, adopted by some of the modern versions, namely, "in coming days" (Berkeley) or "in days to come" (Revised Standard Version), must be considered excellent.

In the passage under consideration (Jer. 30:24) the context is also abundantly clear. Note *"After seventy years are accomplished for Babylon* I will visit you . . . and I will bring back your captivity [or: will restore your fortune] . . . and you will be my people, and I will be your God. . . . The fierce anger of Jehovah will not turn back until he will have executed and accomplished the intents of his heart. *In the latter days* you will understand this"* (Jer. 29:10, 14; 30:22, 24). It is very clear, therefore, that the phrase "in the latter days," as here used, indicates that when Jehovah's judgments have been fully executed, and the seventy years will have ended, God's people will understand that his punishment had been inflicted in order to heal them.

It has become clear, therefore, that none of the aforementioned passages (Isa. 11:11, 12; Jer. 29 and 30; Zech. 8:1-8) has anything whatever to do with a twentieth century A.D. return and restoration. Neither do any of the other passages: Deut. 30:1-10; I Kings 8:46-52; Jer. 18:5-10; Ezek. 36:17-19, 26-28, 33; and Hos. 11:10, 11. They all speak of divine judgments and restorations that had significance for the people who were living at the time when these prophecies were uttered. *In their literal sense* they were intended for *them* and for *their* children, grandchildren, and so forth, not for the people living today, though it is true that their underlying moral and spiritual lessons remain valid for every generation:

> "Let children thus learn from history's light
> To hope in our God and walk in his sight,
> The God of their fathers to fear and obey,
> And ne'er like their fathers to turn from his way."

No. 149 of *The Psalter Hymnal of
the Christian Reformed Church*,
centennial edition, third stanza;
cf. Ps. 78:1-8

Answer to 6. Now if the Old Testament does not contain any predictions regarding a present-day return of the Jews, then, of course, by implication it does not teach either that their present return *in unbelief* is a fulfilment of prophecy. In fact, such a return, namely, *in unbelief*, is not even predicted with respect to the deliverance from the *Assyrian-Babylonian* exile! It is worthy of note that those who have accepted the idea of such a return *in unbelief* offer hardly anything that might even superficially pass as scriptural proof. Even such a passage as Ezek. 36:24-26 is, of course, no proof. The Lord, through Ezekiel, does not say, "I will bring you into your own land, *and then afterward* I will give you a new heart." He simply mentions two things he will do for his people, without immediately stating the order in which these events will follow each other. If the context sheds any light at all on the sequence of events, it would rather seem to place spiritual cleansing — hence, repentance and faith — *before* re-establishment as a nation, though both occur in the same "day," a day of indeterminate length. Note verse 33: "Thus saith Jehovah, In the day that I cleanse you from all your iniquities, I will cause the cities to be inhabited, and the waste places to be builded."

This sequence of events, so that returning to Jehovah *precedes* restoration, is, in any case, the regular order that we find in Scripture. *God does not reward disobedience but obedience.* Hence, the deliverance predicted in the prophets is *conditional* in character. What the prophets meant when they predicted recovery from the Assyrian-Babylonian captivity was this: "Israel will be restored *if it repents.* In that case its sins will be blotted out, and it will be permitted to return to its country."

See this for yourself by consulting the references that were indicated a moment ago:

"And it shall come to pass *when* thou shalt return unto Jehovah thy God, that *then* Jehovah thy God will turn thy captivity" (Deut. 30:2, 3).

"Jehovah will again rejoice over thee for good, *if* thou return unto Jehovah thy God with all thy heart" (Deut. 30:9, 10).

"*If* they shall bethink themselves in the land whither they are carried captive, and make supplication to thee saying, We have sinned, and have done perversely, we have dealt wickedly, *if* they return unto thee with all their heart and with all their soul in the land of their enemies who carried them away captive, *then* hear thou their prayer and their supplication, and forgive thy people, and show them compassion" (I Kings 8:47-50).

Jeremiah 18:5-10. Here the Lord states that *whenever* he predicts that *woe* will befall a nation, then *if* that nation repents, he will also "repent" of the evil which he had intended to do to it. On the other hand, *whenever* he predicts *weal* for any people, then *if* that people becomes disobedient, he will "repent" of the good which he had intended to do to it. A definite rule is established here, showing that there is, indeed, a sense in which we can call the divine impartation of blessing a *conditional* matter. It must always be born in mind, however, that it is only by God's grace and power that men are able to fulfil the condition. But the condition is there, nevertheless. We have no right to take these "*ifs*" out of the Bible! Note, therefore, the words: "*If* that nation turn from their evil, I will repent of the evil that I thought to do to them" (Jer. 18:8). Observe that, here in Jer. 18:5-10, the Lord himself declares that *whenever* he predicts weal or woe, good or evil, for a nation, the condition *always* applies. It would therefore also apply to a passage like Jer. 31:35-37, though there are those who in their explanation of that passage forget all about Jer. 18:5-10.

Hosea 11:10, 11 was also mentioned. Here, too, as elsewhere, *repentance precedes return and restoration!* We read, "They shall walk after Jehovah . . . and the children shall come trembling from the west . . . out of Egypt . . . and out of the land of Assyria." (This, by the way, presupposes that Assyria was still in existence. Where is it today?) A noted commentator has the following comment on the Hosea passage: "As a result of divine love, now actively displayed, Israel will return from the exile. The Lord has placed himself at the head, and those who return will gladly follow him, for they have been cured of their desire to depart from him" (J. Ridderbos).

Answer to 7. It has now become clear that the establishment of the state of Israel, May 14, 1948, *in unbelief* — for those who established it are still rejecting the Christ — "has nothing whatever to do with divine prophecy."[10] This is true for two reasons: (a) Prophecy says nothing about a twentieth-century return and restoration; and (b) even if it did, it speaks about a return *of a believing remnant.*

That the spirit of repentance was actually present at the time of the return from the Assyrian-Babylonian captivity is clear from such passages as the following: Dan. 9:1, 2, 5, 6; Ezra 3:5, 10, 11; 6:16-22; 7:10; 8:35; 10:11, 12; Neh. 1:4-11; Hag. 1:12, 13, etc.

Answer to 8. It has also become clear that *inasfar as passages like Isa. 35:1; 61:4 and others refer to physical and economic restoration*, they, too, have reference to the times of the recovery from the Assyrian-Babylonian captivity. In Isaiah

---

[10]G. Ch. Aalders, *De Oud-Testamentische Profetie En De Staat Israel,* p. 18.

there are over forty references to Assyria, the Assyrian, and the Assyrians. Babylon and the Chaldeans are mentioned about twenty times. Cyrus, who gave orders for the rebuilding of the temple at Jerusalem, is mentioned in 44:28 and 45:1. The nations upon whom judgments are pronounced in Chapters 13-24 are Babylonia, Assyria, Philistia, Moab, Syria, Ethiopia, Egypt, Arabia, Edom, and Phoenicia. All this suits the old dispensation, not the twentieth century A.D.

That during the years intervening between the return from captivity and the birth of Christ there were indeed periods when the desert "blossomed as the rose [or crocus]," is clear from passages in Josephus and in I Maccabees. The former speaks of "renovation of former prosperity," and "cultivation of the land"; the latter about "tilling the land in peace," "the land giving its increase," and "each man sitting under his vine and fig tree" (cf. Micah 4:4). It is, accordingly, entirely unnecessary and unwarranted to transfer the *literal* fulfilment of such and similar prophecies to the twentieth century A.D.

Answer to 9. Was Amos (9:14, 15) actually speaking about the twentieth century A.D. "state of Israel"? Where, in the entire Bible, whether Old or New Testament, does the Lord pinpoint present-day states, telling us exactly what will happen and what will not happen to them? The writer well remembers a series of articles that appeared in a religious journal, now defunct, during World War II. Detailed predictions were made, all of them purportedly *on the basis of prophecy.* One of them was that Italy would emerge as *the winner!* There was wide demand for these articles. But history itself gave the lie to this line of interpretation. This holds, too, for the writings of those who claim the ability to foretell what is going to happen to such countries as Germany, Russia, China, and the United States of America, all, it is claimed, *on the basis of Holy Writ!* That such prognostications are popular was to be expected. Mankind is incurably inquisitive. To the extent to which this curiosity is focused upon that which God has actually revealed, it is an inestimable blessing. But when this desire to know everything goes beyond the limits indicated in Deut. 29:29 it is no longer a blessing at all. Did not even Plato hold that there is some vice of impiety in enquiring too curiously about God and the world? When inquisitiveness becomes intrusiveness, when curiosity degenerates into nosiness, watch out! In the past, too, there have been those who predicted confidently that it would be utterly impossible to destroy "Israel" (by whatever name the political unit was then known) or Jerusalem with its temple. See Jer. 7:4; also Josephus, *Wars of the Jews* VI.v.2. But Jerusalem fell in 586 B.C., and again in A.D. 70, and again in A.D. 135.

Answer to 10. By no means all dispensationalists or similarly minded people are agreed that today Jerusalem is no longer being trodden down. Are not the circumstances with reference to this city still rather insecure? Even R. Wolff is of the opinion that the expression "trodden down" (Luke 21:24) could refer to contemptuous ill treatment (*op. cit.,* p. 53), which, as is well-known, continues to this very day. And as to the idea that the return of the ancient city to the custody of the Jews means that "the times of the Gentiles" have now been fulfilled, in the same issue of *Christianity Today* (Dec. 22, 1967, insert. p. 19) in which this is suggested the opposite view is also expressed; see the issue itself — not the insert —, p. 35. Here we are told that the consensus is that "the times of the Gentiles" will not be concluded until the second coming of Christ. The meaning, then, is simply this, that Jerusalem and those whom it represents will be trampled underfoot during the entire lengthy span of time that extends to the moment of Christ's return. The treading down by the Gentiles will not stop before the close of the present era. Moreover, there is no implication here, or anywhere else in Scripture, of any literal restoration of Jerusalem *after* the second coming.

To be sure, the passage speaks of a being trodden down *until* —. But it just is not true that in every case in which *until* is used this little word introduces a condition which is the exact opposite of that which was described in the preceding part of the sentence. Merely on the basis of what is stated here in Luke 21:24 it is certainly not possible to conclude that earthly Jerusalem as we now conceive of it, or the people whom it represents, will be entering a condition of un-clouded, radiant glory at Christ's return. That little conjunc-tion (*until*) must be interpreted, in each case, according to its specific context. Here in Luke 21:24 the meaning is simply this, that for Jerusalem the condition of being trampled under-foot *will not cease* a hundred years or fifty years or even ten years before Christ's return, but will last on and on and on, *until* Christ's second coming. Somewhat similar is the mean-ing of this little word in Rom. 11:25; I Cor. 11:26; 15:25; and Rev. 2:25. The fact that each passage must be studied in its own context is clear especially from this last mentioned text. Does "That which you have, hold fast *until* I come" actually mean that after Christ's coming we shall no longer hold fast the precious spiritual treasures that have been im-parted to us? Does it not rather indicate that, *come what may,* we must keep clinging to God's revelation in Jesus Christ and to its fruit in our own experience? Relinquish it? Never! Not today, nor tomorrow, nor the next day. We must *hold it fast* — *by giving it away* to the nations!

It is clear, therefore, that neither the word *until* nor any-thing else in this passage is or implies a prediction of national restoration in store for the Jews either just before or in con-nection with Christ's return.

Let us suppose for a moment that another temple will be built in the state of Israel. Will it be a temple in which the Jews will gather in order to glory in the cross of Christ? Cf. Gal. 6:14. If not, then will not the restoration of such a temple constitute further evidence of the fact that the divine ap-proval is not resting upon such worshippers? Was it not our Lord Jesus Christ who said, "I am the way and the truth and the life; no one comes to the Father but by me" (John 14:6; cf. Matt. 1:21; Acts 4:12; Heb. 10:12, 14; Rev. 7:14)?

Answer to 11. This concerns Matt. 19:28. In answer to Peter's question, "Look, we have left everything, and followed thee, What then shall we have?" Jesus says, "I solemnly declare to you who followed me, that in the reborn universe when the Son of man shall sit on the throne of his glory, you will also sit on twelve thrones, judging the twelve tribes of Israel."

It is immediately clear that this prediction does not in any sense refer to what is happening in the twentieth century A.D. Nor does it refer to anything that is still to happen before the one and only second coming of Christ to judgment. The reference is clearly to what will take place in the new heaven and earth, the restored universe. See Matt. 25:31 ff.; Rev. 21:1, 5; and compare Isa. 65:17; 66:22; and II Peter 3:13. What we have here is the solemn assurance that those who have sacrificed most (note: "We have left everything") will receive a special measure of glory. More than many others they will share in the glory of their Redeemer. Passages like I Cor. 15:41b, 42a; II Tim. 2:12; Rev. 3:21; 20:4 shed light on the nature of this reward. Those who have been most loyal to Christ *here* will be closest to him *there.* Within the sphere of "the twelve tribes" special honor and dignity will be accorded to those who have placed their all on the altar of devotion. The expression "the twelve tribes of Israel" refers, according to F. W. Grosheide,[11] to "the restored new Israel . . . the entire people of God." Whether, as such, it indicates the total number of the elect gathered out of the twelve tribes from the beginning to the end of the world's history (cf. Rom. 11:26), or even *all* the chosen ones out of both the Jews and the Gentiles (cf. Gal. 6:16), in either case it must refer to those who have been regenerated, for into the reborn universe of which Matt. 19:28 speaks nothing unclean will ever enter (Rev. 21:27). It is immediately apparent,

---

[11]See his *Kommentaar op het Nieuwe Testament, Mattheus,* p. 232, on this passage.

therefore, that there is here no mention of any massive return of the Jews to Palestine followed by national conversion.

Answer to 12. I Cor. 10:32 reads as follows "Give no occasion for stumbling, either to Jews, or to Greeks, or to the church of God." The apostle Paul, in his characteristic manner, is exhorting the Corinthians to impose upon themselves a voluntary restriction in the use of Christian liberty. He does not want them to throw stumbling-blocks in the path of *anybody*. Not only with respect to "the church of God," should believers watch their conduct, giving none of its members just cause for offense, but they must exercise the same circumspection and tender regard toward *others*, namely, Jews and Greeks. Note that in this passage the Jews are not mentioned in connection with the church of God, as if the apostle had in mind two elect groups. On the contrary, the *Jews* are mentioned in connection with the *Greeks* ("Gentiles," Authorized Version), as together constituting the body of non-Christians. The meaning, therefore, is this: "Be devoid of offense for non-Christians (whether Jews or Greeks) as well as for Christians." The non-Christians are divided into two classes: Jews and Greeks. That this is, indeed, the correct view is indicated by the very terminology that is used here. On the one hand, in order to indicate the two divisions of the first group Paul uses two terms of exactly similar structure: both are *plural* nouns: "Jews and Greeks"; while, on the other hand, the *singular* noun "the church" is used to refer to the second group. The passage, therefore, simply shows that Paul makes a clear distinction between (a) unbelievers and (b) the church of God; and that, with reference to (a), he distinguishes between unbelieving Jews and unbelieving Greeks. *In no sense whatever does he conjoin Jews and the church, as if both of these were objects of God's very special delight.* There is, accordingly, nothing in this passage that will give any comfort to those who expect a return of the Jews to Palestine, followed by conversion!

It has been made clear, therefore, that the view according to which recent happenings prove that the Lord is fulfilling ancient prophecies regarding the return and restoration of the Jews is an error. One more matter must be briefly stated before this chapter is finished:

As was stated previously, the various predictions of restoration for Israel were fulfilled in the return from the Assyrian-Babylonian exile, *inasfar as they were intended to be fulfilled in a literal sense.* It remains true, of course, that the *literal* fulfilment of these and of similar prophecies of weal does not exhaust their meaning. Ultimately these predictions are fulfilled in Christ, and therefore also in all those, whether Jew or Gentile, who place their trust in him. For more on this see Chapter IV.

CHAPTER III

IS GOD FINISHED WITH THE JEWS?

It has been established that the restoration predictions have no reference to what is happening today on a national scale or will take place in the future. Explained in their own literary and historical contexts these prophecies do not refer to any twentieth century (or later) national return in unbelief, followed by national conversion, and so forth. Does this mean that God is finished with the Jews? Those who, contrary to all New Testament teaching (Matt. 8:11, 12; Rom. 10:12, 13; I Cor. 7:19; Gal. 3:9, 29; Eph. 2:14, 18; Col. 3:11; I Thess. 2:14-16; I Peter 2:9; Rev. 2:9), maintain that the Jews are still God's specially favored people, and that the program of their future glory is already beginning to unfold, sometimes speak as if with respect to this subject there are only two alternatives: (a) *their* view, and (b) the view that "God is finished with the Jews," as if all Jews were doomed forever. But is it not possible to reject both of these extremes, and to accept a third position? Instead of accepting a future *national* conversion of the Jews, is it not possible to believe in *remnant* conversion? And, instead of limiting this conversion to the *close* of the dispensation, is it not better to connect it with *every* period of history until the return of the Bridegroom, when at last the door will be shut against those who are not ready to enter (Matt. 25:10)?

These questions remind one of the *remnant* passage, Rom. 11:5, "Even so then at this present time also there is a remnant according to the election of grace," which, in turn, is a fitting introduction to 11:26a: "And so all Israel shall be saved." But since Rom. 11:26a is often quoted in connection with Gal. 6:16, a brief discussion of the latter must precede.

Gal. 6:16

"And as many as shall walk by this rule, peace [be] upon them and mercy. . . ." According to the preceding context, the *rule* in question is the one by which only *this* is of consequence, namely, that a person places his complete trust in Christ Crucified, and that, therefore, he regulates his life by this principle. This means that his life will be one of gratitude and Christian service out of love for his wonderful Savior. Upon those — *all* those and *only* those — who are governed by this rule *peace and mercy* are pronounced. So far the interpretation runs smoothly. A difficulty arises because of the last phrase of this verse. That last phrase is: "*kai* [in the original] upon the Israel of God." Now, varying with the specific context in which this conjunction *kai* occurs, it can be rendered: *and, and so, also, likewise, even, nevertheless, and yet, but,* etc. Sometimes it is best left untranslated. Now when, here in Gal. 6:16, this conjunction is rendered *and* (as in Authorized Version, American Revised Version, and New English Bible), it yields this result, that after having pronounced God's blessing upon all those who place their trust exclusively in Christ Crucified, the apostle pronounces an additional blessing upon "the Israel of God," which is then interpreted to mean "the Jews," or "all such Jews as would at some future time be converted to Christ," and so forth. I cannot accept this translation. It tends to make Paul contradict his whole line of reasoning in this epistle. I show this in detail in my *New Testament Commentary on Paul's Epistle to the Galatians.*

Here I need say only this, that, in harmony with all of Paul's teaching in this epistle (and see also Eph. 2:14-22), and also in harmony with the broad, all-inclusive statement at the beginning of verse 16, where the apostle pronounces God's blessing of peace and mercy upon "as many as" shall walk by this rule, it is my firm belief that those many translators and interpreters are right who have decided that *kai,* as here used, must be rendered *even,* or (with equal effect) must be left untranslated. Accordingly, what the apostle says is this: "And as many as shall walk by this rule, peace [be] upon them and mercy, *even* upon the Israel of God." Cf. Psalm 125:5. Upon all of God's true Israel, Jew or Gentile, all who truly glory in the cross, the blessing is pronounced. This rendering, according to which *kai* is either translated *even,* or is left untranslated, is also favored by the following: The Amplified New Testament, Berkeley Version, Calvin, Erdman, Lenski, Lightfoot, Phillips, Rendall, Revised Standard Version, and Williams. John Murray is correct when in his (*New International*) *Commentary on Romans* (Vol. II, pp. 9 and 10) he states that in Gal. 6:16 the expression *the Israel of God* includes "the people of God of all nations."

It is clear, therefore, that what was true in connection with Matt. 19:28; Luke 21:24; and I Cor. 10:32 holds also with reference to Gal. 6:16: none of these passages predict the return of the Jews to Palestine in unbelief, followed by conversion.

And so we arrive at the final passage, namely,

Romans 11:26a

"And so all Israel shall be saved."

This text occurs in the section Romans 9-11, which forms a unit. The connection between it and the preceding chapter is very remarkable. That glorious chapter — Romans 8 — ends with a shout:

"Nay, in all these things we are more than conquerors through him that loved us. For I am persuaded that neither death, nor life, nor angels, nor principalities, nor things present, nor things to come, nor powers, nor height, nor depth, nor any other creature, shall be able to separate us from the love of God which is in Christ Jesus, our Lord." It is a song of triumph, a shout of victory.

But hard upon this we hear a tone that is altogether different. It is a plaint of sorrow and pain wrung from a tempest-tossed heart:

"I say the truth in Christ, I lie not, my conscience bearing witness with me in the Holy Spirit, that I have great sorrow and unceasing pain in my heart. For I could wish that I myself were anathema from Christ for my brethren's sake, my kinsmen according to the flesh. . . ."

How is this striking contrast between the paean of praise and the confession of heartache to be explained? To us it seems most probable that the connection between the rapture and the lamentation is emotional rather than merely intellectual. Paul may have meditated on this wise: "What treasures of joy are bestowed on those who love God: the Spirit makes intercession for them (8:26); so does Christ (8:34); hence, believers are more than conquerors (8:37-39), and yet . . . many of my own 'brethren' fail to share in these glorious blessings. And they . . . the people of the promise! Has the promise of God come to nought then? God forbid!" Now reread the opening verses of Chapter 9. Paul's self-disclosure throbs with emotion. It is characterized by a kind of effervescence. The words fairly seethe. The style is animated. The most profound and glorious thoughts are, as it were, crowding each other. When one idea is touched upon, another, equally rich and penetrating, is already pressing forward for recognition. Paul has dipped his pen in the ink of truth *and love!* He pours out his heart, beginning as follows:

"For I could wish that I myself were anathema from Christ, for my brethren's sake, my kinsmen according to the flesh." In the history of literature, is there anything more stirring? We see Paul, the born Jew, taking his stand with Moses, who cried out: "Yet now, if thou wilt forgive their sin . . . ; and if not, blot me, I pray thee, out of thy book which thou hast written."

Has God's promise come to nought? Has God become unfaithful? Perish the very thought! Nevertheless, how is it possible to reconcile God's promises to Israel with Israel's unbelief and consequent rejection? That this question underlies the entire argument is evident from passages like the following: "But it is not as though the word of God has come to nought" (9:6); "I say then, did God cast off his people?" (11:1).

Paul — inspired by the Holy Spirit — answers as follows:

(a) The rejection of Israel is *not complete;* "But it is not as though the word of God has come to nought. For they are not all Israel that are of Israel" (9:6). This, among other things, is taught in Chapter 9.

(b) The rejection of Israel is *not arbitrary.* It was Israel's own fault. The way of salvation had been made perfectly plain to the Jews. Their sin was that of wilful and stubborn unbelief: "But as to Israel he saith, All the day long did I spread out my hands unto a disobedient and gainsaying people" (Rom. 10:21). This is the emphasis in Chapter 10.

(c) The rejection of Israel is *not absolute and unqualified.* There is also a glorious promise; "And so all Israel shall be saved" (11:26a). This is the conclusion of the argument in Chapter 11, resuming the thought of Chapter 9.

Now there are those who regard these three chapters as embodying contradictory answers. One author tells us that it is "the climax of pathetic absurdity" to attempt to harmonize the two contradictory conceptions of God which underlie these chapters. How can we think of God as, on the one hand, holding out his hands in tender and persistent pleading all through the day, and yet, on the other hand, with those same outstretched hands hardening those over whom he was yearning? As if God would not be just when he hardens those individuals who had rejected such tender, yearning love! Let us return to the promise of Rom. 11:26a: "And so all Israel shall be saved." Just what is the meaning of these words? That is the question to which we shall try to discover the answer.

Now, the answers to this question vary greatly. First, there are those who interpret the term "all Israel" as referring to the entire number of the elect from the Jews and Gentiles, i.e., the church (Calvin, Van Leeuwen and Jacobs). Others see in this passage a promise of restoration for Israel as a people. In this group there are first of all those who refer "all Israel" to the Jewish people collectively, some (not all) interpreters being careful to emphasize that not necessarily every Jew living in the end-time will be saved; thus, some dispensationalists; also Denny (*Expositor's Greek Testament*), Doekes, Erdman, Gifford, Greijdanus, Hodge, Sanday and Headlam (*International Critical Commentary*), Shedd, Van Andel, Voigt, Vos. Others, however, fear too many qualifications and restrictions, and boldly teach that all living Israelites who will not have been converted before the endtime will then be saved (Meyer and many dispensationalists), some even opining that those Jews who have already died will be raised in order to share in Israel's national conversion. Finally, there are those who adopt the position that the term "all Israel" refers to the total number of elect Jews (Barthing, Bavinck, Berkhof, Hallesby, Lenski, Odland, Herman Ridderbos, and Volbeda).

For the purpose of simplification it is, perhaps, best to limit ourselves to the discussion of the three main answers which have been given:

1. *"All Israel" indicates the entire people of God: the total number of the elect out of both Jews and Gentiles; that is, the church.*

John Calvin in his *Commentary on Romans* states: "*And so all Israel, etc.* Many understand this of the Jewish people, as though Paul had said that religion would again be restored among them as before: but I extend the word *Israel* to all the people of God, according to this meaning, 'When the Gentiles shall come in, the Jews also shall return from their defection to the obedience of faith; and thus shall be completed the salvation of the whole Israel of God, which must be gathered from both; and yet in such a way that the Jews shall obtain the first place, being, as it were, the first-born in God's family.' This interpretation seems to me to be the most suitable, because Paul intended here to set forth the completion of the kingdom of Christ, which is by no means to be confined to the

Jews, but is to include the whole world. The same manner
of speaking we find in Gal. 6:16. The Israel of God is what
he calls the Church, gathered alike from Jews and Gentiles;
and he sets the people, thus collected from their dispersion, in
opposition to the carnal children of Abraham, who had de-
parted from his faith."

Substantially the same view is found in *De Brief aan de
Romeinen* (*Korte Verklaring der Heilige Schrift met Nieuwe
Vertaling*) by J. A. C. Van Leeuwen and D. Jacobs: "The
term 'all Israel' must be understood as indicating those who
are called out of the Gentiles together with the remnant of
Israel."

2. *"All Israel" refers to the Jews as a people or collectively.*
Here let me quote from another excellent commentary, that
by S. Greijdanus, *De Brief van den Apostel Paulus aan de
Gemeente te Rome* (*Kommentaar op het Nieuwe Testament*):

"The term 'all Israel' in this connection can hardly mean
anything else than Israel as a whole, over against a small
portion formerly, and over against those upon whom a hardening in part has fallen. Whereas formerly only a relatively small
number of Jews became believers, and the greater number
were hardened, being exposed to that sentence, this is going
to change after the fulness of the Gentiles is come in. Then
Israel as a whole, the Jewish people collectively, will come to
conversion and to believing acceptance of the Gospel of God
in Christ, the Lord."

3. *"All Israel" indicates the full number of the elect from
among the Jews; in other words, the remnant.* Says H.
Bavinck in his *Gereformeerde Dogmatiek* (third ed., Vol.
IV, p. 744):

"Accordingly, the term 'all Israel' does not indicate the people of Israel which will be converted on a large scale in the
end-time; neither does it refer to the church out of Jews and
Gentiles; but it is the pleroma which, in the course of cen-

turies, is gathered out of Israel." (The translation of the last three quotations is my own — W. H.)

We shall, accordingly, study these three answers in the order given. What is meant by "all Israel" to which this glorious promise is given? Is it (a) the church? Is it (b) the Jews collectively? Or, is it (c) the elect remnant of the Jews?

1. Beginning, then, with the first view, according to John Calvin and some eminent present-day commentators the term "all Israel" in Rom. 11:26 refers to the church. Let no one think lightly of this interpretation. Let no one ridicule it. Calvin was the greatest commentator of his day. Even today his commentaries are read with much profit. Much, indeed, can be said in favor of Calvin's explanation of Rom. 11:26.

First of all, let it be observed that the idea as such that the elect gathered out of Jews and Gentiles constitute *one* people, and shall be saved, is emphatically scriptural. Nowhere in the entire New Testament do we find the view that God has two favored peoples — the Jews on the one hand, the church on the other — and that these two differ in calling (earthly versus heavenly), in ethical norm or standard, in way of salvation (vision versus faith), and in future glory (the Jews forever on earth, the church forever in heaven).

Secondly, not only is Calvin's idea scriptural but, in addition, it is brought out in the immediately succeeding context of the passage which we are considering. Verses 30-32 read as follows:

"For as you in times past were disobedient to God, but now have obtained mercy by their disobedience, even so have these also now been disobedient, that by the mercy shown to you they also may obtain mercy. For God has shut up all unto disobedience, that he might have mercy upon all."

Thirdly, not only in the verses just quoted but again and again in the epistles of Paul do we find the idea of the *one* church, comprising the entire company of the elect out of Jews

and Gentiles. It is a definitely Pauline conception. See Rom.
10:12, 13 — occurring, therefore, in this very section. See also
Gal. 3:28; Eph. 2:14.

Fourthly, there are those who argue that the immediately
preceding context of our passage favors Calvin's interpretation
with respect to Rom. 11:26a. The reasoning of these commentators is as follows: in verses 23 and 24 Paul speaks about
the "grafting in again" of the natural branches; i.e., of the
Jewish remnant. In verse 25 he adds to this remnant the
pleroma (fulness or full number) of the Gentiles. Then follows: "And so *all Israel* shall be saved." The conclusion to
which these interpreters arrive is that the term "all Israel"
indicates the remnant of the Jews plus the full number of
elect from among the Gentiles.

Fifthly, Calvin refers to Gal. 6:16 in support of his interpretation of Rom. 11:26a. We have already seen that in that passage the term "the Israel of God" refers, indeed, to all the
elect out of all the nations.

Calvin's interpretation is by no means easily refuted. Hence,
it does not surprise us that it has present-day supporters among
the most eminent conservative exegetes, who have written
splendid commentaries.

Nevertheless, it does not *wholly* satisfy us. It is, perhaps, not
entirely correct. It is correct insofar that it ascribes a
spiritual connotation to the term *Israel* as here used. But
does "Israel" here in Rom. 11:26a indicate the church gathered out of Jews *and Gentiles?* That is the question. Con-
siderations may be advanced against each of the arguments
on which the view of Calvin and of those who agree with
him rests.

With respect to the first, second, and third arguments it may
be said that they do not furnish solid evidence that here in
Rom. 11:26a the term "all Israel" means the whole body of
believers whether Jew or Gentile. It is one thing to observe
that *the idea* of a Church universal is scriptural and Pauline.
It is a different matter to prove that the term "all Israel"

has that meaning. And it is an altogether different matter to establish the point which must be established; namely, that this term has that meaning in *this* particular context.

For the moment passing by the fourth, let us turn at once to the fifth argument. It furnishes perhaps, the strongest support for Calvin's view. The passage at least teaches us that Paul, as well as the Old Testament, is not unfamiliar with the definitely *spiritual* connotation of the term *Israel* and at times employs the term in a spiritual sense. It is, perhaps, not erroneous to say that the term "the Israel of God" in Gal. 6:16 and the term "all Israel" in Rom. 11:26a are alike insofar that both refer to *spiritual* Israel. The individuals comprised under either term are true believers. This, however, does not yet prove that the two slightly different terms have *exactly* the same meaning. It is *possible* — whether it is also *probable* we shall consider later — that while the term "the Israel of God" in Gal. 6:16 refers to the whole body of believers gathered out of Jews and Gentiles (as has been established), the term "all Israel" in Rom. 11:26a refers to the whole body of *Jewish* believers.

This brings us to the crucial point: the context of Rom. 11:26a. Now, a moment ago we pointed out that according to those who favor Calvin's view the preceding context supports his interpretation. See the fourth argument as described above. They reason that the term "all Israel" is the result of an addition: the remnant of Israel plus the pleroma of the Gentiles equals "all Israel." But at this point the weak element in Calvin's view becomes apparent. Says Doekes:

"In these three chapters [Romans 9-11] the term 'Israel' occurs no less than eleven times. And in the preceding ten cases it refers indisputably to the Jews, in contrast with the Gentiles. What compelling reason can there be, therefore, to accept another meaning here? Not, to be sure, the context, for the differentiation between Jews and Gentiles does not cease in verse 25 but is continued in the verses which follow. Nor is the meaning of the term 'Israel' altered by the prophecy which Paul introduces in support of the truth expressed, witness the purposely quoted names 'Zion' and 'Jacob.' "[12]

The fact that Paul, in the entire context, is speaking about Jews when he uses the term "Israel" becomes evident immediately when all the passages are examined in which that term is used. Notice:

"For I could wish that I myself were anathema from Christ for my brethren's sake, my kinsmen according to the flesh: who are *Israelites* . . . and of whom is Christ as concerning the flesh, who is over all God blessed forever. Amen" (9:3-5).

"For they are not all *Israel* [the spiritual seed of Jacob, for explanation see Gen. 32:28] that are of *Israel* [the physical seed]" (9:6).

"And Isaiah cries concerning *Israel*, If the number of the children of *Israel* be as the sand of the sea, it is the remnant that shall be saved" (8:27).

"What shall we say then? That the Gentiles, who followed not after righteousness, attained to righteousness, even the righteousness which is of faith: but *Israel*, following after a law of righteousness, did not arrive at that law" (9:30, 31).

"But I say, Did *Israel* not know?" (10:19).

"But as to *Israel* he says, All the day long I spread out my hands unto a disobedient and contrary people" (10:21).

"I say then, Did God cast off his people? God forbid. For I also am an *Israelite*, of the seed of Abraham, of the tribe of Benjamin" (11:1).

"What then? That which *Israel* seeks for, that he obtained not . . ." (11:7).

". . . a hardening in part hath befallen *Israel* . . ." (11:25).

It is, therefore, reasonable to conclude that when in the very next verse the apostle again uses the same term, he is still thinking of Jews, as in every previous instance throughout these three chapters. Hence, when Calvin assigns the meaning "church" to "all Israel" this is probably incorrect; at least, partly incorrect.

---

[12]*De Beteekenis van Israëls Val,* p. 892.

Again, it is not at all likely that Paul is here adding, so that "all Israel" would be the sum of the remnant of the Jews and the pleroma of the Gentiles. On the contrary, the immediately preceding context — verses 23 and 24 — concerns the *Jews*, not the Gentiles. Says Paul, in verse 23, "And they also (i.e., the Jews) if they continue not in their unbelief, shall be grafted in: for God is able to graft them in again." So also in verse 24: "if thou . . . how much more shall *these* [again, these Jews] be grafted into *their own* olive tree?" Follow verse 25, which again concerns the Jews: "a hardening in part has befallen *Israel*." It is true that at the end of the verse "the pleroma of the Gentiles" is mentioned but it is referred to only in order to indicate that the hardening of the *Jews* shall last until every elect Gentile shall have been brought into the kingdom. Paul, therefore, is still talking about the Jews. Hence, when he now continues: "And so *all Israel* shall be saved," it becomes evident that this term "all Israel" cannot refer to the church universal. Paul, clearly, is still speaking about Jews. He does so also in the succeeding context, as is clearly evident; verse 26b: "He shall turn away ungodliness from *Jacob*."

As we read on, we notice that Calvin's difficulties increase. Also verse 28 contains a clear reference to the Jews: "*they* are enemies for your sake." It is not until the apostle reaches verses 30-32 that he causes the whole body of elect, Jew and Gentile alike, to pass in review together, as we have indicated previously.

We should be careful in interpreting the term *Israel*. In Rom. 11:26a it in all probability does not indicate the church universal. It has reference to Jews, not to Gentiles.

2. But this does not necessarily mean that Calvin was *all* wrong. It is possible that his interpretation contains a valuable element of truth. For, it being established that the term "all Israel" refers to Jews and not to Gentiles, the next question is: Does it refer to (a) the people of the Jews as a whole; in other words, the physical unit; or does it signify (b) the

entire Jewish remnant that is gathered into the fold of God throughout the centuries, according to the election of grace? On the surface, the term "all Israel" is conceivable for either connotation.

Now, the former view is widely held. It has been accepted by earnest Bible students of various orthodox groups. They define "all Israel" as meaning "the Jewish people," or "Israel as a nation," or "Israel as a whole . . . the Jewish people collectively," or "the whole nation," or "the great mass or body of the nation who are to be converted after the evangelization of the Gentile world," or "the totality of the people . . . the Jews on a very large scale," or "large numbers of Jews," or "enough of the Jews to represent the race."

Some link this interpretation of Rom. 11:26a with their conception of God's entire program for the future of the Jews: their return to the land of the fathers, their exaltation to a place of political prominence, and their significance for the evangelization of the human race. According to these dispensationalistic interpreters the Jews not only will be saved but will become the saviors of the world. They will be the channel through which the gospel of grace reaches the world in the age of ingathering.

But others are far more conservative in their interpretation of Rom. 11:26a, and confine their theory to the belief that the great mass or body of the Jews will be converted after the evangelization of the Gentile world and just before or in connection with the second coming of the Lord.

At any rate, whatever be the difference in detail, most of the interpreters whose view we are now discussing agree that the term "all Israel" refers to the great mass of the Jewish people.

What shall we say with respect to this view? One thing is certain: the theory contains an important element of truth. This has already been indicated. Romans 9–11 deals with a problem touching the Jews. Of that there can be no further doubt. The term "all Israel" in Rom. 11:26a has reference to Jews, not to Gentiles.

Is the theory true in its entirety, however? Does Rom. 11:26a refer to the entire physical group or does it refer to the spiritual remnant? That is the question.

Now, in order to do justice to the arguments advanced by those who take the term "all Israel" as indicating the whole mass of the Jews, we cannot limit ourselves to an examination of Paul's argument in the immediate context of the passage under discussion. The reason is this: those who defend this view constantly appeal in support of their conclusion to (a) Old Testament prophecy; (b) the Gospels; and (c) the entire Section Romans 9–11; at least Chapter 11. Hence, in order to follow their argument we shall have to say something about these three matters.

(a) The line of argumentation *from prophecy* is somewhat as follows: *The Old Testament contains promises concerning the restoration and implied conversion of the Jewish nation.*

But before the restoration passages culled from the Old Testament can be adduced as evidence in support of a restoration of the Jewish people in and after the twentieth century A.D., it must be convincingly shown that these passages have not been fulfilled in the past. In Chapter II it has already been shown that the Old Testament nowhere predicts a twentieth century, and so forth, restoration.

(b) The appeal to the Gospels (for example, to Matt. 19:28; Luke 21:24) fares no better, as has also been indicated, namely, in Chapter II, answers to 10 and to 11. Our Lord was according to the flesh, a Jew. He was a son of Abraham, Isaac, Jacob, and Judah. He loved the Jews. He wept over Jerusalem. If the Jews as a nation are to be restored, Jesus would have said so. He never did. He *did* say:

"If thou hadst known in this day, even thou, the things which pertain unto thy peace! but now are they hid from thine eyes. For the days shall come upon thee, when thine enemies shall cast up a bank upon thee, and compass thee round, and keep thee in on every side, and shall dash thee to the ground, and thy children within thee; and they shall not leave thee one stone upon another; because thou knewest not the time of thy visitation" (Luke 19:43, 44).

(c) But have the proponents of the idea that Rom. 11:26a promises a future restoration to the Jewish nation a right to appeal to the teaching of Paul elsewhere; i.e., in passages other than Rom. 9—11? Does the apostle teach this in I Cor. 10:32 or in Gal. 6:16? In this treatise it has already been shown that in these passages he teaches nothing of the kind. Nor does he teach it anywhere else. Observe also the following:

First of all, it is a significant fact that among those who endorse the view which we are discussing there are some who admit that elsewhere Paul rejects the idea of a future national conversion of the Jews. Their reasoning is as follows: Paul contradicts himself. Here, in Romans 11 he is teaching something which in I Thess. 2:15, 16 he has emphatically rejected. Says C. Lattey in *St. Paul and His Teaching*:

"From Rom. 11:25-32 we learn of another sign that is to precede the end of the world, the conversion of the Jews; that is, of at least the great mass of the nation. . . . In I Thess. 2:15, 16, St. Paul appears to be far from the expectation of such a conversion."

Yes, Paul was, indeed, far from such an expectation in I Thess. 2:15, 16: ". . . the Jews . . . who both killed the Lord Jesus and the prophets, and drove us out, and please not God, and are contrary to all men; forbidding us to speak to the Gentiles that they may be saved; to fill up their sins always; *but the wrath is come upon them to the uttermost.*"

A better solution of the difficulty is that Romans 11 is in perfect agreement with I Thess. 2:15, 16, and that neither passage teaches a still-future national conversion.

Secondly, according to the very uniform teaching of Paul, special privileges for any definite national or racial group have ceased during the new dispensation. His words are clear and simple.

"For there is no distinction between Jew and Greek: for the

same Lord is Lord of all, and is rich toward all that call upon him: for whosoever shall call upon the name of the Lord shall be saved" (Rom. 10:12, 13). A still-future period of special spiritual glory for the Jews, as a people, to be ushered in after the last Gentile has been converted, seems hardly in keeping with Paul's oft-repeated teaching about the unity of the church.

Thirdly, it is argued that the term "Israel" in Rom. 11:26a must have the same meaning as in the preceding verse. There is an element of truth in this argument, as we have already pointed out. To a certain extent, the term does have the same meaning in both verses. In both cases it designates the Jews. But is it correct to say that the term must have *exactly* the same meaning in both verses? Not at all. In fact, in this very section — Rom. 9–11 — Paul uses the term "Israel" twice in one verse (Rom. 9:6); yet, in the first instance it indicates the spiritual seed of Jacob (believing Jews), in the second the physical seed (Jews in general). The passage referred to reads: "For they are not all Israel that are of Israel." Now, in Rom. 11:25, 26, the apostle states positively what he stated negatively in Rom. 9:6.

Fourthly, those who favor the still-future national conversion idea introduce a temporal concept into Rom. 11:26a, as if it read: "And *then* — i.e., after the fulness of the Gentiles has come in — all Israel shall be saved." Can anyone conceive of such a situation? But even regardless of the awkwardness of the entire idea, this is not at all what Paul actually says. He says: "And *so* all Israel shall be saved." He is speaking about God's glorious *method* in saving Israel's remnant, a method so glorious that it fills the apostle's soul with rapture and adoration, to which he gives expression in the words of verse 33. That very verse proves that Paul is not thinking about the *time* but about the *way* or *manner* in which "all Israel" is saved.

Moreover, it is not even correct to say that verse 27 points to a definite moment of time (the moment of or just before the second coming). Literally Paul says: "and this for them

the covenant from me *whenever* I shall take away their sins."
See Isa. 59:20, 21; Isa. 27:9. *Whenever* God in his mercy
removes the sin of a Jew, the covenant is realized in his
heart and life.

Fifthly, most of those who adopt the theory under discussion connect this future mass-conversion of the Jews with the
second coming of the Lord. But the immediately following
context clearly connects the salvation of "all Israel" with the
first coming and its effects in the *present* dispensation. Says
Paul, verse 26:

    "and so all Israel shall be saved: even as it is written,

    There shall come *out of Zion* the Deliverer;

    He shall turn away ungodliness from Jacob."

The very fact that this Deliverer comes "out of Zion" and
not "out of heaven" indicates that the apostle is thinking of the
first and not of the second coming. It is as the result of this
first coming that "all Israel" is saved. Paul is speaking throughout these chapters of that which is *now* (in his own day) going on and will continue to take place throughout this dispensation until "all Israel" shall have been gathered in.

God's promise with respect to Israel is being partly realized
in the salvation of Paul himself, and Paul is living *now;* i.e.,
when these words were written (11:1). It is as if Paul had
said: "Do you wish proof that God is actually faithful to his
promise to save Israel? Well, look at me! He saved me, and
I am an Israelite."

In this connection the words of 11:5 are very significant:
"Even so then *at this present time* also there is a remnant
according to the election of grace."

Paul is *even now* striving to be an instrument in God's hand
for the salvation of Israel's remnant (Rom. 11:14).

Study also Rom. 11:31: "even so have these also *now* been
disobedient, that by the mercy shown to you, they also may
now obtain mercy."

It is evident, therefore, that the salvation of "all Israel" was
being progressively realized in Paul's own day and age, and
that it will continue to be progressively realized until "all

Israel" shall have been saved. When the full number of elect Gentiles will have been gathered in, then the full number of elect Jews will also have been gathered in.

Finally, if here in Rom. 11:26a Paul is speaking about a still-future *mass*-conversion of Jews, then he is overthrowing the entire carefully built-up argument of Chapters 9—11; for the *one* important point which he is trying to establish constantly is exactly this, that God's promises attain fulfilment not in the nation as such but in the remnant according to the election of grace.

We conclude, therefore, by saying that the widely-held theory that the term "all Israel" refers to the Jewish people *as a whole* is incorrect. The correct element in the theory is this, that the term does, indeed, refer to Jews, though not to the whole nation.

3. What, then, does Rom. 11:26a actually mean, and what is meant here by "all Israel"?

Calvin was partly right and so are those who differ with him. Calvin was right in believing that the term "all Israel" refers to those who trust in the Lord. He was right in giving a spiritual connotation to the term. Those who differ with him are right in declaring that the term refers to Jews, and not to Gentiles. After what has already been said little evidence needs to be added to prove that the term refers to *the full number of elect Jews whom it pleases God to bring into the kingdom throughout the ages until the very day when also the full number of the Gentiles shall have been brought in.* "All Israel" is "the remnant according to the election of grace" (11:5). For additional evidence that this is correct we submit the following:

First of all, this view is in harmony with the whole argument of Chapters 9—11. It might seem to some that God had completely rejected his ancient covenant people. This, however, raised a problem: Was it true, then, that God had become unfaithful to his promises to Israel? "No," says Paul, as it were, "but you must remember that even during the old dispensation these promises were intended to be realized only in the lives of true believers.[13] The rest were hardened. But there was always 'a remnant according to the election of grace.' At the present time there is *also* (see 11:5) a remnant. The hardening is not complete, though it might at times seem to be. But it *is* not (11:25). In fact, throughout this entire dispensation, until the very time when the full number of elect Gentiles shall have been gathered into the church, elect Jews will be saved. 'And so all Israel shall be saved.' "

Secondly, this view is also in harmony with the fact that throughout Chapters 9–11 Paul is speaking about *the remnant* (9:27; 11:5). That thought occurs again and again. This remnant is defined as being the true *Israel* (9:6); *the children of the promise* (9:8); *a seed* (9:7, 29); *those on whom God has compassion* (9:15); *his people whom he foreknew* (11:2); *true believers* (10:11); *the seven thousand men in Elijah's time* (11:4); *and the many that were added since his day,* i.e., *the remnant according to the election of grace, which remnant exists also at this present time* (11:5); *those that were chosen* (11:7); *those Jews that continue not in their unbelief but accept Christ by faith and are "grafted in again" as branches into the olive tree* (11:23); *all Israel* (11:26a). For Old Testament remnant passages, see I Kings 19:18; Isa. 1:9; 10:20-22; 11:11, 16; 46:3; Jer. 23:3; 31:7; Joel 2:32; 5:15; Amos 5:30; Micah 2:7, 12; 4:5-7; 7:18; Zeph. 3:13.

It is significant that Paul here quotes some of these very passages (Rom. 9:27; 9:29; 11:4). His "remnant" doctrine is, therefore, by no means a *novelty.*

Thirdly, this interpretation also does justice to the word "all" in "all Israel." The other view does not do justice to it. The apostle does not say that Israel shall be saved on a very large scale; but he says that "all" Israel shall be saved. This "all" clearly indicates *the total number* of elect Jews, without a single exception: *all* the elect. In Elijah's day there was a remnant. In Paul's day there was a remnant. In the years to

---

[13]See what was said earlier on Jer. 18:5-10 (in Chapter II).

come there would be a remnant. These remnants of all the ages, taken together, constitute "all Israel." So also "the fulness of the Gentiles" indicates the total number of Gentiles that are saved.

Finally, this view also gives meaning to the word "so" which introduces the passage: and *so* all Israel shall be saved. This "so" must be interpreted in the light of the immediately preceding context. That context tells us that the hardening which has come upon Israel is not complete, and that throughout this dispensation it never will be. That was the *mystery* which Paul knew by revelation. Hence, in *every* age until the last elect Gentile is saved there will also be Jews who, by sovereign grace, accept Jesus as their Lord and Savior, "and *so* all Israel shall be saved." "So," i.e., by the abiding grace and mercy of God who, though, in punishment for sin, he hardens, does not harden all; "so," hence, through faith. What a wonderful mystery this is! How full of meaning for every age; also, for our own day.

If the mass of the Jews is being punished so severely for rejecting the Christ, how shall we, who have received far greater privileges, escape if we reject him?

If throughout this whole dispensation this process of hardening is but partial, so that there is ever a remnant according to the election of grace, what an incentive this is to the work of evangelization among the Jews!

How the revelation of this mystery fills our hearts with adoration. It had been revealed to Paul that God would bring about the salvation of "all Israel" in a most wonderful manner; a manner, in fact, so very wonderful that *the very rejection of the mass of Israelites, instead of making void the promise of God, would be a link in the fulfilment of that promise;* on this wise, as Paul reasons:

(a) Carnal Israel "falls." It is rejected because of its unbelief. Result:

(b) The gospel is brought to the Gentiles, and the elect Gentiles are saved. Result:

(c) God uses this salvation of the Gentiles to stir up the elect remnant of the Jews to holy jealousy. Result:

(d) The Jewish remnant, too, accepts Christ by faith, in accordance with God's eternal plan.

In every case it is God himself who brings about these results.

But let us quote Paul's own words. See Rom. 11:11, 31:

(a) "By their fall

(b) "salvation is come to the Gentiles

(c) "to provoke them [Israel] to jealousy; so that

(d) "by the mercy shown to you [Gentiles] they [Israel] may now obtain mercy."

Now, is not this just too wonderful for words? Think of it: the very rejection of the Jews, by means of various links, results, by God's sovereign mercy, in the salvation of "all Israel."

Now we can understand why Paul concludes his presentation of this entire matter by exclaiming:

"O the depth of the riches both of the wisdom and of the knowledge of God! How unsearchable are his judgments, and his ways past tracing out! For who has known the mind of the Lord? Or who has been his counsellor? Or who has first given to him, and it shall be recompensed to him again? For of him, and through him, and unto him, are all things. To him be the glory forever. Amen."

It has become very clear, therefore, that the proposition, "God is finished with the Jews," is an error. God has his elect people among the Africans, the Indian tribes, the French, the Dutch, the Mexicans, the Argentinians, the Australians, and so forth, and so forth; and certainly also, he has his elect among the Jews!

CHAPTER IV

ACCORDING TO SCRIPTURE, WHAT IS MEANT BY "ISRAEL"? IS IT TRUE THAT THE BLESSINGS PROMISED TO ISRAEL ARE FOR THE JEWS, NOT FOR THE CHURCH?

A recent issue of a religious periodical contains the statement: "It seems evident that there is no reason to speak of the church as Israel."

Language of this kind has been heard before. In a thesis for the Th.M. degree, written many years ago, the writer of this treatise has quoted a good many statements by various authors who take this position.[14]

Is there any truth in it? There is, indeed, *some,* but the proposition needs to be carefully qualified. It is true that it is wrong to identify Israel, that is, the Jews considered as an ethnic entity, with the visible church of the new dispensation, or with the invisible church of either or both dispensations. There are numerous passages in the Old Testament in which the term *Israel* refers to the Jews as a nation or people, a theocracy. We read that the children of Israel murmured against Moses and Aaron in the wilderness (Exod. 16:2); that a census was taken of the people of Israel (Exod. 30:12); that the people of Israel were made to drink the pulverized golden calf (Exod. 32:20); that the people of Israel offered willingly to Jehovah (Exod. 35:29); that the Lord gave his statutes and ordinances to Israel (Ps. 147:19), and so forth. The Old Testament contains divine promises which, in their literal application, were meant for the Israel-

---

[14]See *The Premillennialistic Conception concerning Israel and the Church,* a copy of which was placed in Calvin Library, Grand Rapids, Mich.

ites, that is, for the Jews. Blessings of a temporal character
are promised to Abraham; for example, "To thy seed will I
give this land" (Gen. 12:7). Also, the promise of Israel's
return from captivity was meant and fulfilled literally, as has
already been indicated.

In the New Testament this literal usage of the term *Israel*
continues. Thus, for example, the statement that an angel
of the Lord tells Joseph to return with his family, from
Egypt to "the land of Israel," does not mean that he must go
to "the land of *the church*." The land of Israel is, of course,
"the land of the Jews." See also Matt. 2:21; 8:10; 9:33;
Luke 4:27; 7:9; John 3:10; Acts 2:22, 36; 3:12; etc.

But alongside of this literal use of the term there is, *from
the beginning*, also a figurative use. Those who say, "the
church is not Israel" frequently fail to give this fact its due.
Yet the very first occurrence of the term "Israel" in Scripture
already implies that a true Israelite is not a person who be-
longs to a certain nation, or one who is able to trace his
ancestry to Abraham, but rather a person who prevails with
God and with men (Gen. 32:28). Note also Psalm 73:1,
"Surely God is good to Israel, even to such as are pure in
heart"; and Psalm 125:5, where the term "Israel" is contrasted
with "those who turn aside to their crooked ways." We are
told that Jehovah will lead the latter forth with the workers
of iniquity. There follows, "Peace be upon Israel." Moreover,
even the *land* promised to Abraham typifies Canaan above
(cf. Heb. 11:10, 16). The *seed* in which all the promises
are focused is Christ (Gal. 3:16).

It is precisely in harmony with such figurative usage that
Paul in Gal. 6:16 pronounces peace upon "the Israel of God,"
a passage that has already been explained. See Chapter III.
That the apostle is not thinking solely of Jews when he uses
the term "the Israel of God" follows also from the immediate
context (verse 15), which reads: "For neither is circumci-
sion anything, nor uncircumcision, but a new creation." The
one and only thing that really matters, says Paul as it were,
is "the new creation," the life of regeneration which the Holy

Spirit brings about in a person's heart (cf. John 3:3, 5; Rom. 2:29). "Faith working through love" (Gal. 5:6) is what counts, not whether a person happens to be Jew or non-Jew. Cf. I Cor. 7:19; II Cor. 5:17. Hence, for Paul the church, consisting of Jews and Gentiles who have accepted Christ as their Lord and Savior, is indeed Israel. We see, therefore, that the proposition, "The church is not Israel," is too absolutistic, too bold. As Paul sees it, the dividing wall between Jews and non-Jews has been broken down through the blood of Christ (Eph. 2:14). The two former mutual enemies have been "reconciled in one body to God through the cross" (Eph. 2:17). *What right have we to rebuild the dividing wall?*

According to Paul not all the descendants of Israel (Jacob) are truly Israel (Rom. 9:6; cf. I Cor. 10:18). Not all are included in "all Israel." See Chapter III on Rom. 11:26a. Not all who are named Jews, after Judah, are true to the implication of that name (Rom. 2:28, 29, with a play on the name *Jew;* cf. John 5:41-44). Not all are those whose praise is from God. Moreover, there are descendants of Abraham who, like Ishmael, were born after the flesh, and there are others who, like Isaac, were born after the Spirit (Gal. 4:29).

But one does not even have to be a physical descendant of Abraham to belong to "the Israel of God" (Gal. 6:16; cf. Rom. 9:24). John the Baptist, too, was fully aware of the fact that physical descent from Abraham does not guarantee being a true son of Abraham. *But he also knew that apart from such descent God can give sons to Abraham* (Matt. 3:9; Luke 3:8).

Now if, therefore, the unqualified statement, "The church is not Israel," is an error, then it is also wrong to affirm, without qualification, that the blessings promised to Israel are not for the church, only for the Jews. The view that blessings formerly promised to the Jewish people are now given to "the Israel of God," namely, to the church of Jew and Gentile, is in harmony with Christ's own teaching. He taught that the privileges which once belonged to the ancient covenant people have been transferred to this new nation.

This is the nation that brings forth the fruits (Matt. 21:43). Many will come from east and west, and will sit down with Abraham, Isaac, and Jacob in the kingdom of heaven; but the sons of the kingdom will be hurled into outer darkness (Matt. 8:11, 12). The vineyard is leased to other tenants (Matt. 21:41). When the invited guests slight the invitation, others from everywhere are brought in (Matt. 22:1-14).

Similarly, Paul plainly states that distinctions pertaining to race, social position, degree of culture, and/or sex, no longer have any significance: "If you belong to Christ, then you are Abraham's seed, heirs according to promise." "Christ is all and in all" (Gal. 3:28, 29; Col. 3:10, 11). Peter stresses the same truth by saying, "You are [God's] elect race, royal priesthood, holy nation, own people" (I Peter 2:9). In other words, the old titles once given to the covenant people of the old dispensation now belong to you.

No one surely will deny that every spiritual blessing is promised to *the church* (Eph. 1:3). That church is Christ's bride (Eph. 5:23, 27, 32). And that bride is at times likened to a beautiful city, Jerusalem the Golden (Rev. 21:2). Yes, the bride is the city (Rev. 21:9, 10). Moreover, upon the gates of that city are written the names of the twelve tribes of Israel, and upon its foundation-stones are inscribed the names of the twelve apostles of the Lamb (Rev. 21:12, 14). Is not this the same as saying that all these blessings are now being bestowed upon the one universal church, the church into which elect from every nation are gathered?

The fact that one day Israel would include the elect from the Gentile-world and that in this world-wide "Israel" God's promises would be fulfilled had already been revealed to the prophets, though not as fully as it was made known to Paul, and so forth, later on (Eph. 3:1-6). The restoration of "the preserved of Israel" (Isa. 49:6) is fulfilled when the gospel is brought to the Gentiles (Acts 13:47). The enlargement of Zion's tent (Isa. 54:1-3) is fulfilled when the Gentiles accept Christ (Gal. 4:27). The new covenant promised by the Lord through his servant Jeremiah (Jer. 31:31-34) is the one which guarantees complete salvation to every believer — whether Jew or Gentile — through simple faith in Christ, apart from all ceremonial ordinances (Heb. 8:8-12; 10:16-20). The symbolism of Ezekiel's healing waters (Ezek. 47; cf. Isa. 44:3; Zech. 14:8) is fulfilled on the day of Pentecost when the Holy Spirit is poured out (John 7:37-39). The prediction according to which those "not pitied" would one day be "pitied," and those who had been called "not my people" would be called "my people" (Hos. 2:23; cf. 1:9, 10) was fulfilled by means of the establishment of the church, considered as the body of those who are called, not from the Jews only but also from the Gentiles (Rom. 9:24-26). The raising up of David's tent (Amos 9:11 ff.) is fulfilled when God visits the Gentiles, to take out of them a people for his name (Acts 15:14 ff.). It is clear, therefore, that there is a sense in which it is entirely proper to say, "The blessings promised to Israel are for the church."

In other words, when a prophecy is destined to be fulfilled in the new dispensation it is fulfilled according to the spirit of that new era. Hence, these Old Testament prophecies are fulfilled in the Spirit-filled church, and there is not the slightest indication anywhere in the Old or New Testament that at some future time the clock will be turned back. Let us begin to breathe the air of the new dispensation. Let us live and think as New Testament people should live and think. Not "Back to Jerusalem!" should be our slogan, but "From Jerusalem into all the world!"

CHAPTER V

WHAT SHOULD BE OUR ATTITUDE TOWARD THE JEWS?

A. *Understanding*

This means that, first of all, we should become thoroughly acquainted with God's revelation with respect to the Jews; as has been set forth in the preceding chapters. This revelation shows us that not only in the closing years of the present dispensation but *always, now* also, there is hope for the Jews: there is that "remnant according to the election of grace" (Rom. 11:5).

Unless we understand the Jews, evangelistic labor among them will be very difficult if not impossible. We should therefore study their history, become acquainted with their religion as it is now being practiced — their emphasis is upon practice far more than upon doctrine — their literature, their likes and dislikes. Not only should we read Christian books about the Jews — of which there are a great many — but also their own books, particularly those in which they set forth their views of us, Christians. Among the latter, one of the most recent and informative is that by S. Sandmel, *We Jews and You Christians* (published by J. B. Lippincott Company, Philadelphia and New York, 1967).

B. *Appreciation*

Wherever and whenever it is possible to do so, without sacrifice of candor, we should appreciate and admire their exemplary traits. Did not even Jesus tell us that the sons of this world are for their own generation wiser than the sons of light? (Luke 16:8). In the affairs of this world these non-Christian people are often shrewder, and we can learn from them. Thus, those who have worked among the Jews have testified that they admire their initiative, thrift, industry, energy, efficiency, partiality for education, and skill. Other valuable traits are respect for parents, emphasis on the importance of the home, and the practice of charity. We should also appreciate the ardent desire of those among them who are earnestly striving to settle the Israel-Arab problem in such a manner that a solution, in the best interest of *all*, may be found, a solution that includes a satisfactory answer to the problem of the Arab refugees!

We should gladly recognize that throughout history Jews have rendered service to mankind in many departments of life. Under God, who gave us our Bible, including our beautiful psalms and inspired prophecies? At Expo-67 on a wall inside the *Israel Pavilion* precious passages from the Psalms, dear to the heart of both Jew and non-Jew, were inscribed in huge letters. The writing was in many languages, and the hearts of all were thrilled. Moreover, is it not true that Jews have been responsible for many advances in the three M's: Mathematics, Medicine, and Music? Perhaps the reader has also been informed about the amazing knowledge of the Old Testament that is being displayed by many of the Israeli boys and girls. O that all the gifts and talents with which these people have been so richly endowed might be applied also — yes, first and most of all — to the service of him who is indeed the true Messiah, King of kings and Lord of lords! O that the veil which prevents them from seeing in the Old Testament the glory of Christ might be taken away (II Cor. 3:15, 16)! Otherwise even such a thing as amazing knowledge, a large store of information, is accompanied by blindness.

C. *Sympathy and Co-operation*

Of course, we should deeply sympathize with the Jews in the losses they have suffered, the persecutions they have endured, sometimes because of their *religion*, at other times because of their *race*. In the name of Christianity — a very

strange brand indeed! — they have been maligned, mal-
treated, and expelled from one country after another. And
for an entirely different reason six million of them — men,
women, fathers, mothers, children, infants — were murdered
by Hitler, a deed of horror that staggers the imagination.

Nevertheless, although nothing should be subtracted from
the emphasis upon the injustice and cruelty of all this, it is
but fair to state that Jews, in their writings, at times forget
that persecution is not a one-way street. As has been shown
— see Chapter I — there is a sense in which it is entirely
correct to state that it was the Jews who killed Jesus. The
book of Acts reveals very clearly how the persecution of
Christians by Jews was carried on in the early church. And
even today this persecution has not ceased, especially toward
Jewish converts to Christianity. A few years ago a newly
converted woman, originally from Poland, remarked, "All our
lives we suffered in Europe because we were Jews. Now we
suffer in Israel because we are Christians."

The answer to all this is Christianity, that is, Christ living
in the hearts and lives of people, so that through the power
of his Spirit true love toward all becomes evident, and co-
operation is no longer a hollow sound but is practiced in
every way.

D. *Eager Desire to Win Souls for Christ,*
to the Glory of God

We are reminded of such passages as:

"He who wins souls is wise" (Prov. 11:30; see, however,
the different translations).

"They that turn many to righteousness [shall shine] as
the stars for ever and ever" (Dan. 12:3).

"Brothers, my heart's desire and my supplication to God
is for them, that they may be saved" (Rom. 10:1).

"I have become all things to all men, that in one way or
another I may save some" (I Cor. 9:22).

What is the attitude of present-day Jews toward Christianity? Missionary work among them has not been wholly un-

fruitful. According to God's promise it will always bear fruit, for *God is not finished with the Jews,* as has been pointed out earlier. Yet such work of Jewish evangelism is not easy. To be sure, tolerance from the side of Jews has been reported. But even tolerance is not conversion. Books and articles have appeared in which Jewish writers reveal this attitude: We, Jews, intend to remain Jews. We are not trying to convert you to our religion. Why are you trying to convert us to yours?[15] A Jewish professor in the United States describes Christianity as a kind of polytheism. Another Jew, H. J. Schonfield, in his paperback, *The Passover Plot,* pictures Jesus as an arch-schemer, who with the utmost skill and resourcefulness plotted his own crucifixion and last minute revival. As to the latter, something went wrong, so that, in spite of detailed devising, the plan miscarried. Further, Schonfield is convinced that the stranger who talked with the two disciples that were on their way to Emmaus was not Jesus, and that the rumor according to which the disciples of Jesus had stolen his body (Matt. 28:13) is true. When will someone write a dissertation that will expose the fallacies contained in *The Passover Plot?* As we see it, the book is the product of a keen mind, a rather detailed knowledge of sources, and a too fertile creative imagination.

The characterization of the religion of the Israelis as being "humanism" or "the religion of labor" may be too generalizing. Nevertheless, still another Jewish writer, Louis Finkelstein, author of the two-volumed work, *The Jews, Their History, Culture, and Religion,* writes with enthusiasm about "the spirit of humanism" which by the Jews was infused into the thinking of fourteenth to seventeenth century Europe. He also makes mention of "the moral autonomy of man over against the Christian doctrine of original sin" (pp. 653, 654 of the above-mentioned work). He tells us that the humanist element was at the bottom of medieval Jewish philosophy

---

[15]See, for example, the statements by S. Sandmel, *op. cit.,* pp. 138, 142.

from its very inception. And does not today's Judaism speak with relish about "the great universal ideals of mankind"?

There are no signs today of a massive return to Palestine followed by conversion. According to the latest statistics the ratio of *a.* the number of Jews in the state of Israel, to *b.* the total Jewish world population, is only slightly better than one to six. As to all the others, three out of every six Jews are to be found in the Americas; the other two elsewhere, mostly in Europe (Russia, etc.). But, as has been shown in Chapter II, even if every Jew should try to crowd into the state of Israel tomorrow morning, this would not be a fulfilment of prophecy!

Of course, it is possible that if the leftist wing of the ecumenical movement has its way, and various large religious groups have become united, having accepted as their common creed "God is the Father of all men, and all men are brethren," some Jews might also join. And it is conceivable that increasingly rabbis may attend consecration ceremonies for Roman Catholic bishops. But, though on the subject of prophecy and its fulfilment we differ with the dispensationalists and their kindred, we credit them with enough doctrinal soundness to discount such "conversions" (?).

Nevertheless, it is nothing less than true repentance and faith in the Lord Jesus Christ that is needed. We should address ourselves to the task of winning the Jews for Christ with something of the self-effacing spirit of Moses (Exod. 32:32), of Paul (Rom. 9:1-5), and above all, of Christ (Matt. 23:37).

We should, of course, preach Christ to them, as the fulfilment of their need of *an atonement by blood.* Some Jews are keenly aware of this lack in their religion as *now* practiced. Furthermore, we must imitate Peter and Paul in showing the Jews that this same Christ is also the fulfilment of the prophecies that are found in their Bible. But none of this will avail unless it be accompanied by fervent prayer, and the power of Christ's resurrection be shown in our own lives. *We should constantly bear in mind that for every Jew who reads the New Testament there are a hundred or more that read us!* During World War II it was especially Christian love that was lavished upon bitterly persecuted Jews by the people of the Netherlands and by others that succeeded in winning many of them for Christ, as they themselves have testified. We must extend to these people a hearty welcome to our homes and to our hearts, and this all the more in view of the fact that conversion to the Christian religion causes them to be treated as outcasts by their former friends and relatives.

Now all this work should be carried on with tact and understanding, as is true with respect to every mission endeavor. More than anything else, we should tell these people *the truth.* The attempt to inspire them with false hope, as if somehow, *in spite* of their rejection of Christ, they are still God's special favorites, is inexcusable. Our Lord wants the Jews to come to *him.* Establishing a home in the state of Israel is not the solution of their deep-seated spiritual problem. Such a trek to the land of the fathers has nothing to do with prophecy and with their salvation. And salvation, to the glory of God Triune, is what the Jews stand in need of most of all, as does every man of every race and nationality, as he is by nature. "For *all* have sinned, and fall short of the glory of God" (Rom. 3:23; cf. 2:11; 3:9-18; 5:12, 18). But also: "The same Lord is Lord of *all,* abounding in riches for *all* who call upon him" (Rom. 10:11, 12).